Holes!

A Coloring Book

This is a **coloring book**,
but not an ordinary coloring book.

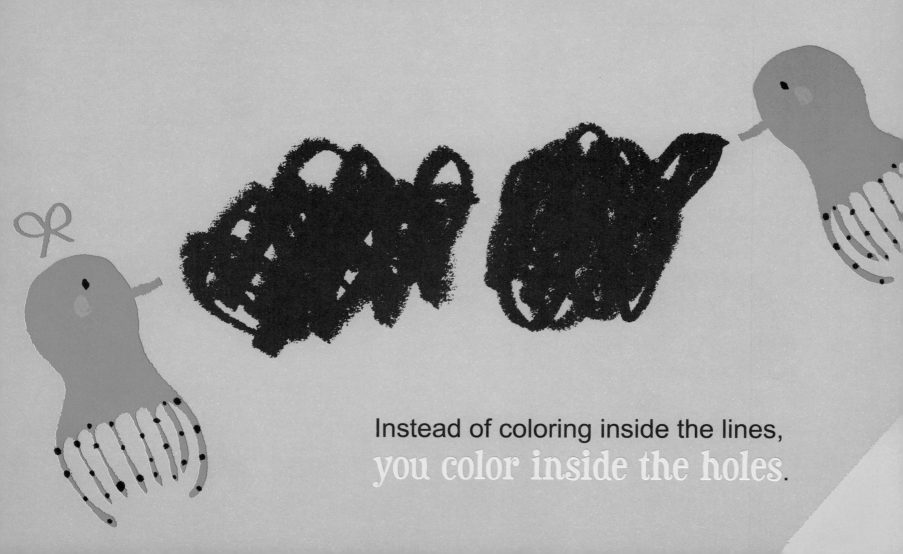

Instead of coloring inside the lines,
you color inside the holes.

You'll find that

what you've colored inside the holes
changes into something else
when you turn the page.

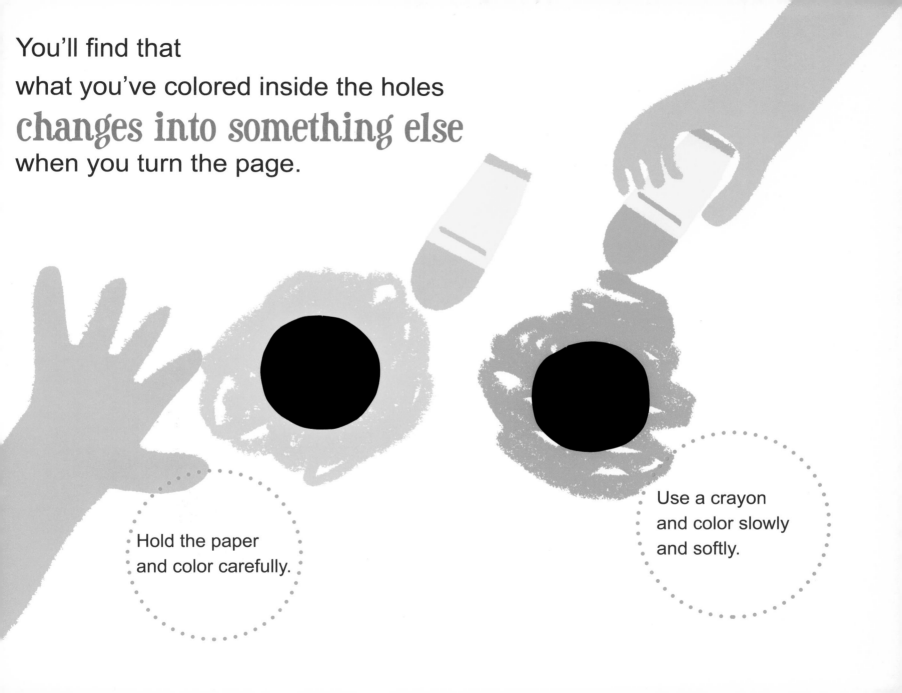

Hold the paper
and color carefully.

Use a crayon
and color slowly
and softly.

Look! The holes became car tires.

Before you know it,
you have a different picture.
It's like **magic!**

Yum!
The holes became ice cream cones.

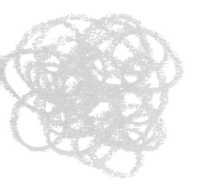

After you color in the holes, you could even draw pictures on the page.

I added a cherry!

Do you see that the ice cream is the color of the hole from the previous page?

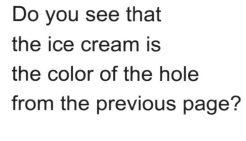

Now it's your turn.
Color the white flowers and make them bright and beautiful.

These flowers have holes.
Use your crayons and fill in the holes on the flowers.

See? The holes turned into butterflies!

Now color the wings of
the butterflies.

Thanks for the cute ribbons!

Color in the holes that look like baseball caps.

What colors do you want
to make the white cars?

The holes shaped like
baseball caps have turned into cars!

Oh, no! There are holes in the sweater.
Color them in red to hide the holes.

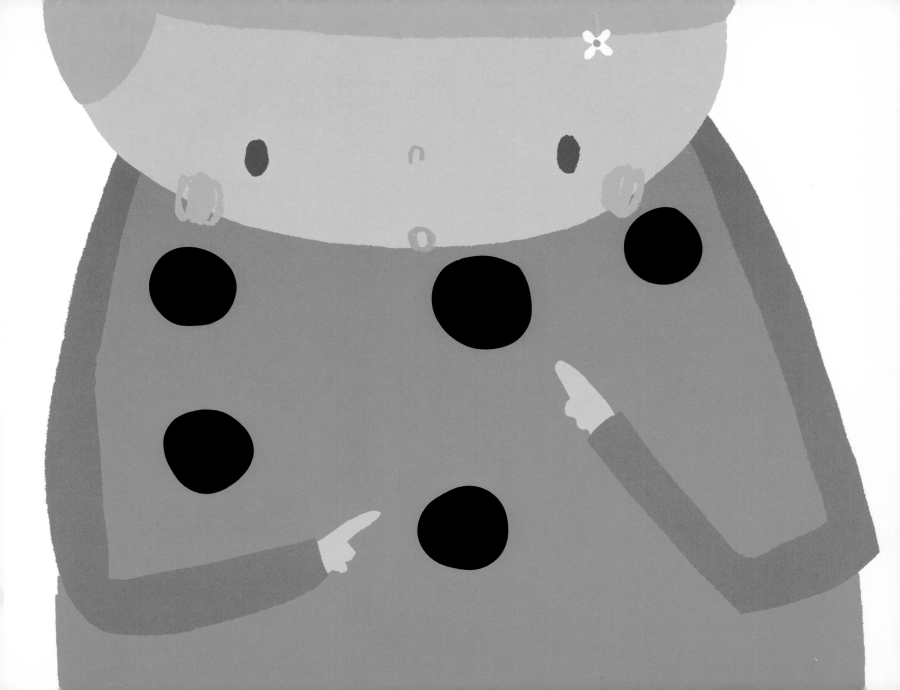

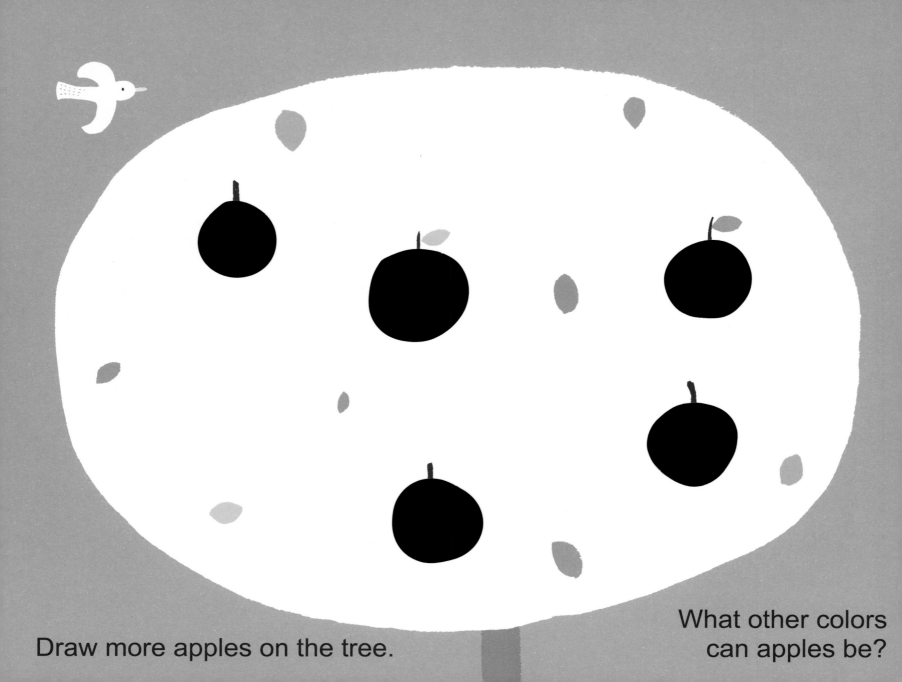

Draw more apples on the tree.

What other colors can apples be?

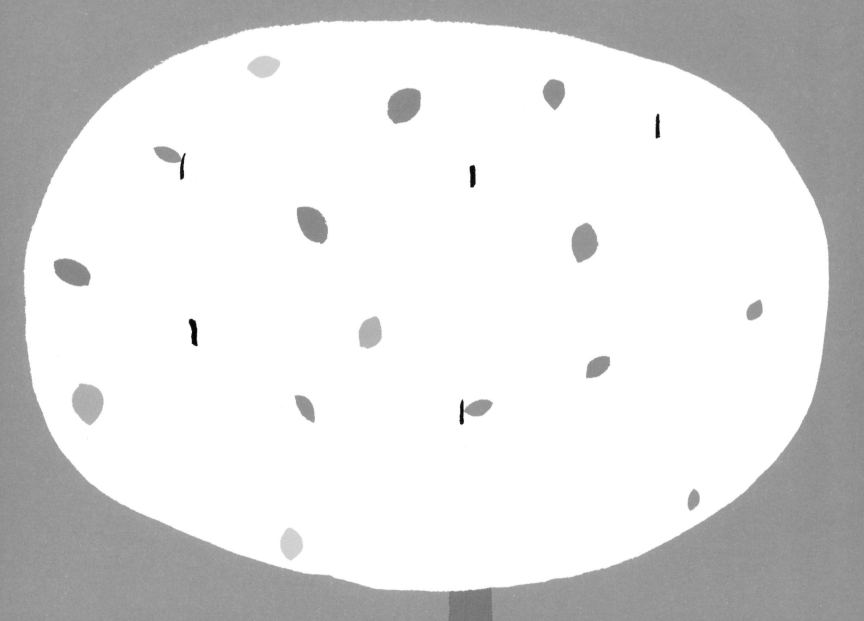

The holes turned into red apples!

Can you color in a square?

Cool! The hole turned into a train!

Trains need to run on tracks.
Can you draw some railroad tracks?

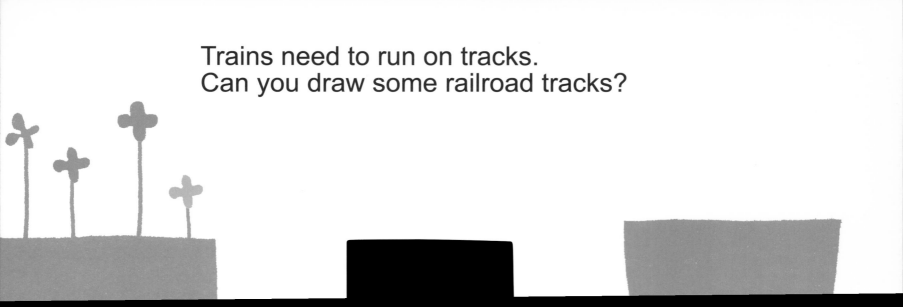

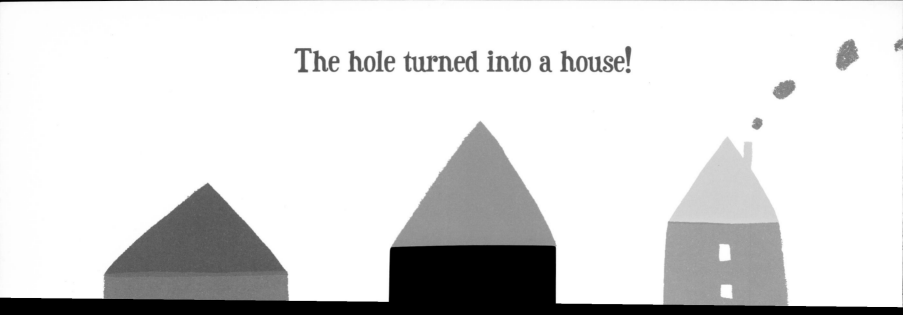

The hole turned into a house!

Draw more flowers around the houses.
What else can you draw here?

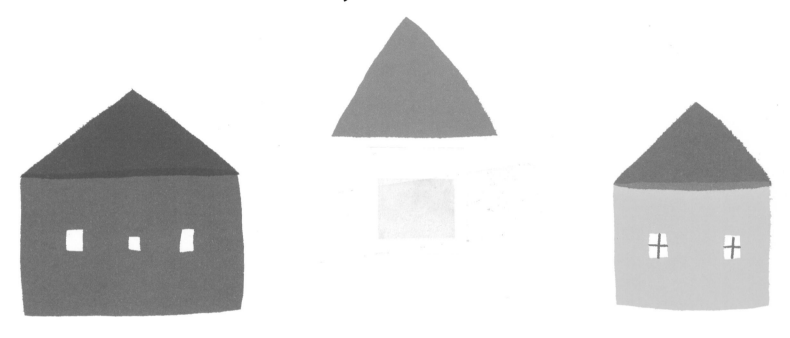

Now the hole has turned into a present.

Draw ribbons on the presents.

Color in the white holes
with a black crayon.

These silly ghosts love the dark.

Draw a tongue
on each ghost.

Thanks for the eyes!

BOO!

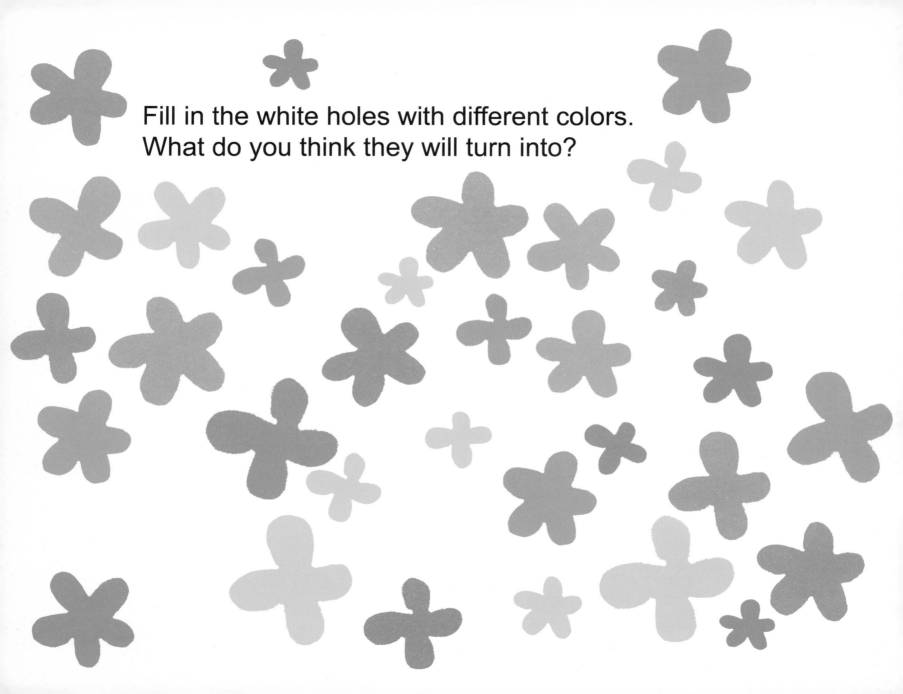

Fill in the white holes with different colors.
What do you think they will turn into?

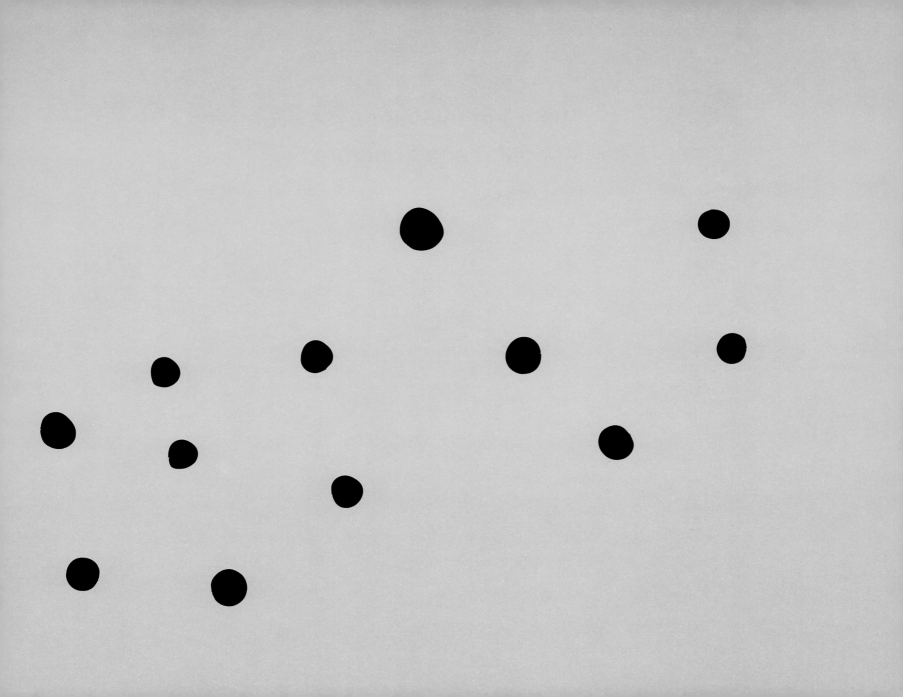

The butterfly has never seen
a spotted snake before.
Have you?

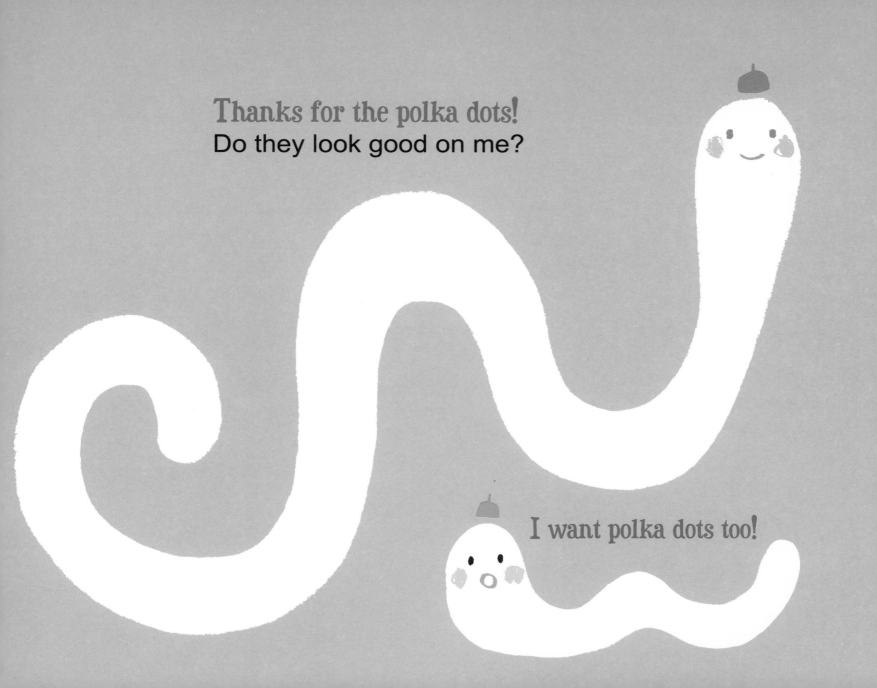

Color in these holes.
What will they turn into?

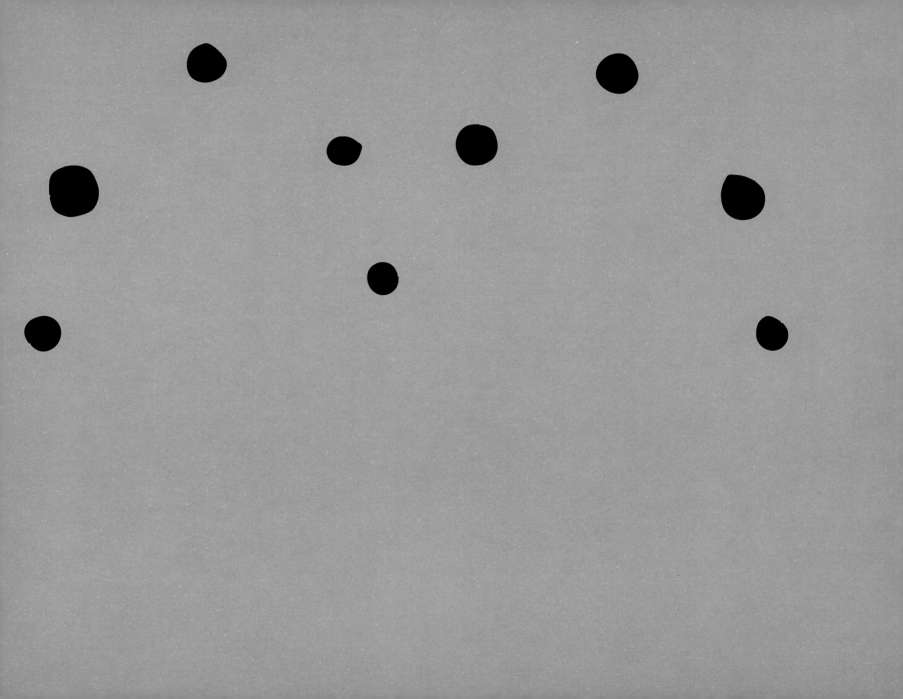

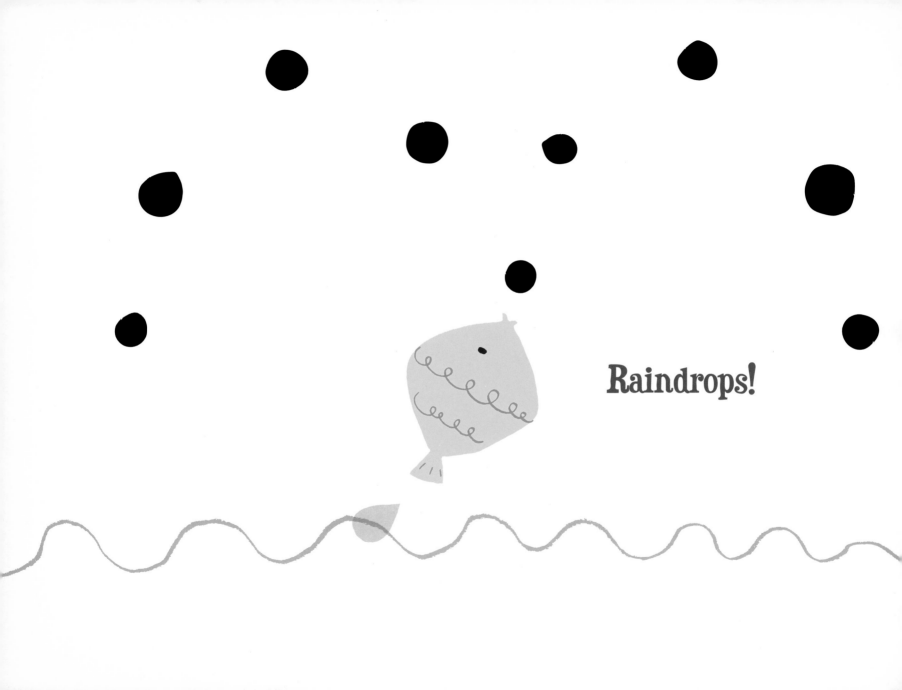

Raindrops!

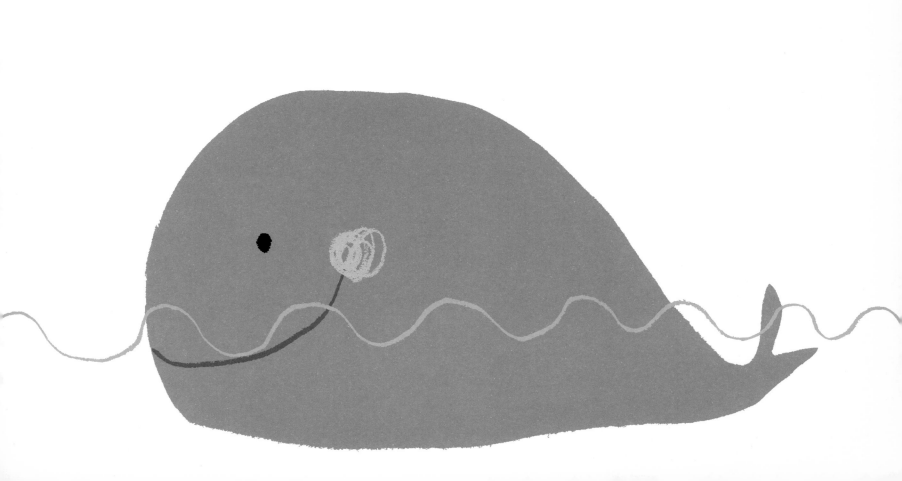

Color the hole shaped like a triangle and turn it into a tree.

The hole turned into a tent!

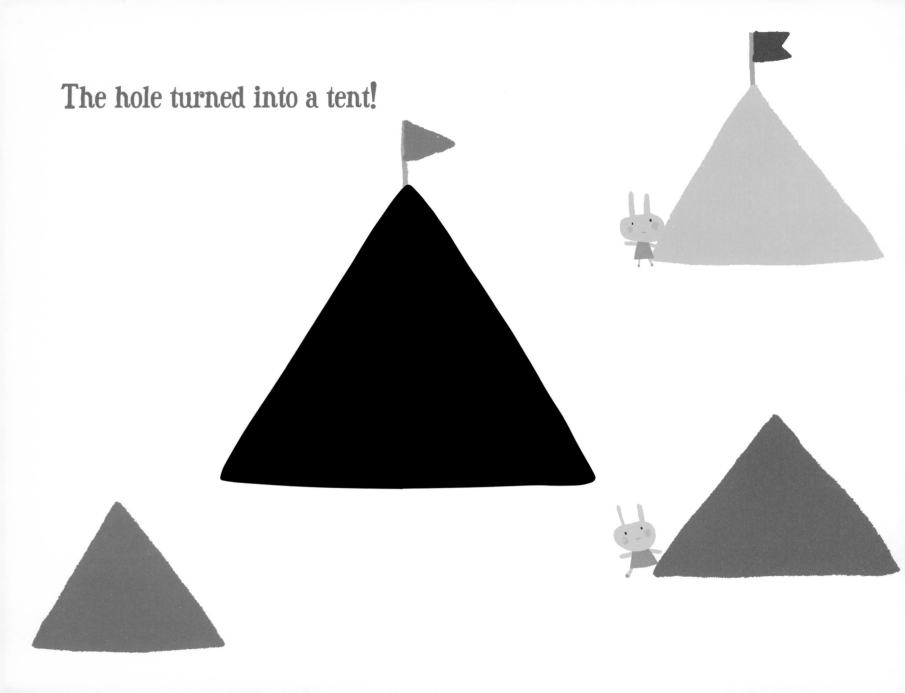

Can you put flags
on the rest of the tents?

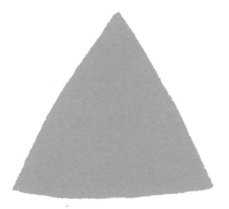

The hole turned into a fish!

Can you fill the pond
with more fish?

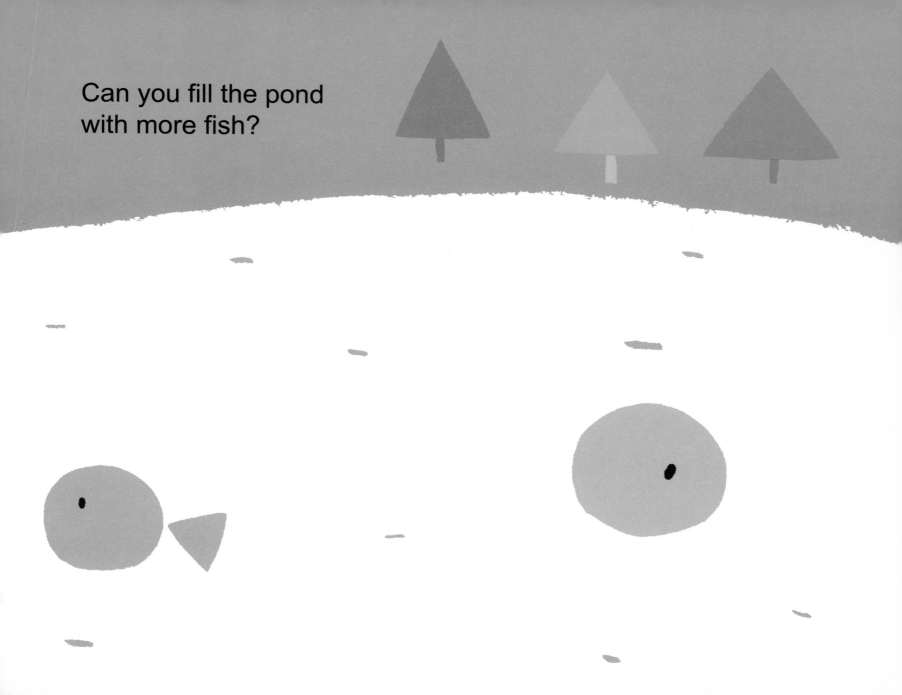

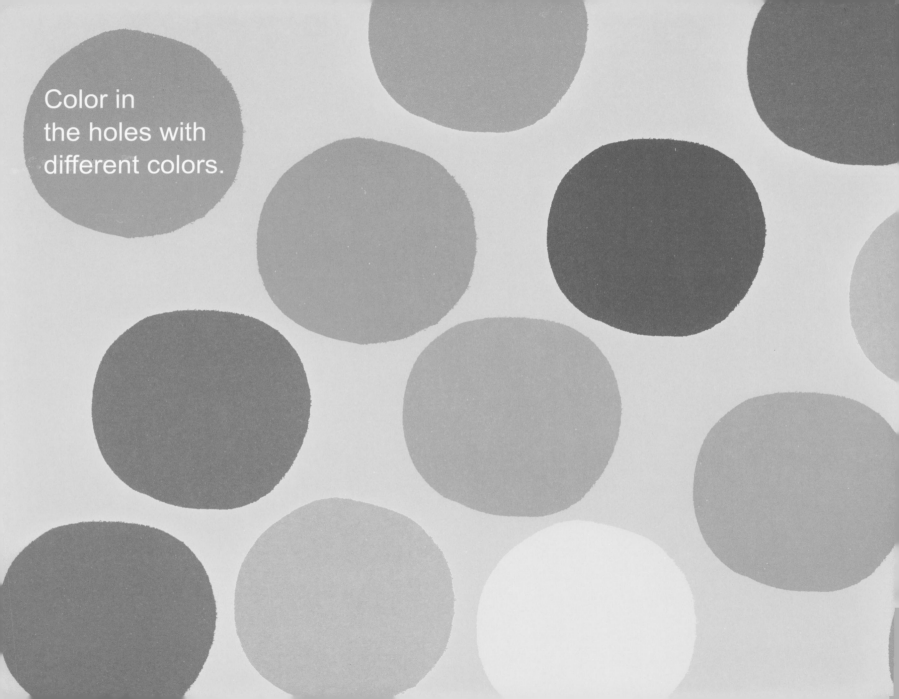

Color in
the holes with
different colors.

Thanks for
making me
such a pretty dress!

A girl octopus and a boy octopus
squirt ink into the hole.
Color in the hole with lots of
circles and curly patterns.

Here I go!

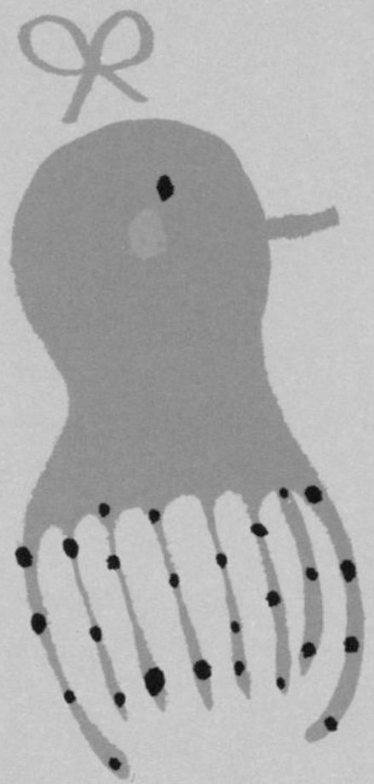

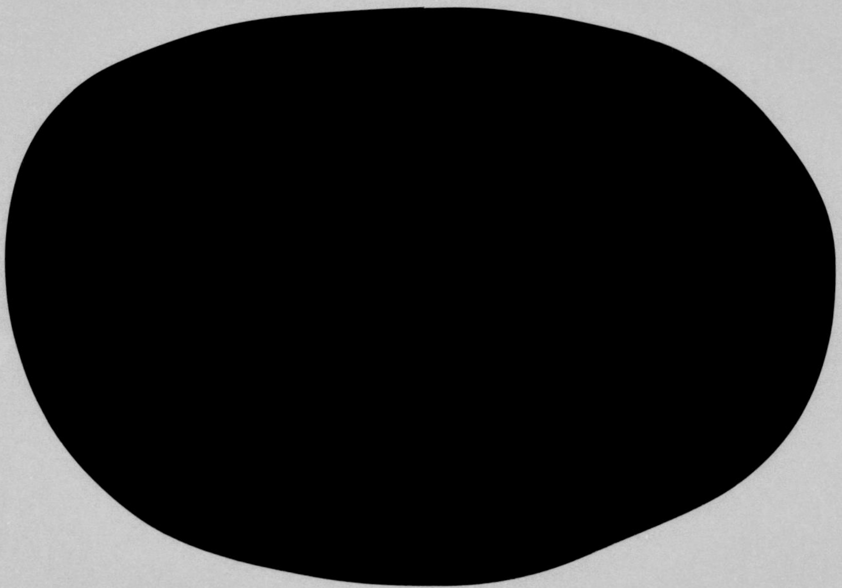

Okay, my turn!

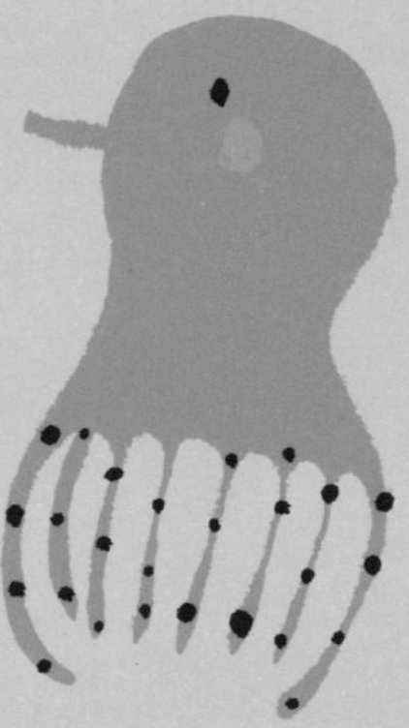

Wow! The ink from the octopus
turned into a silly mustache and beard!

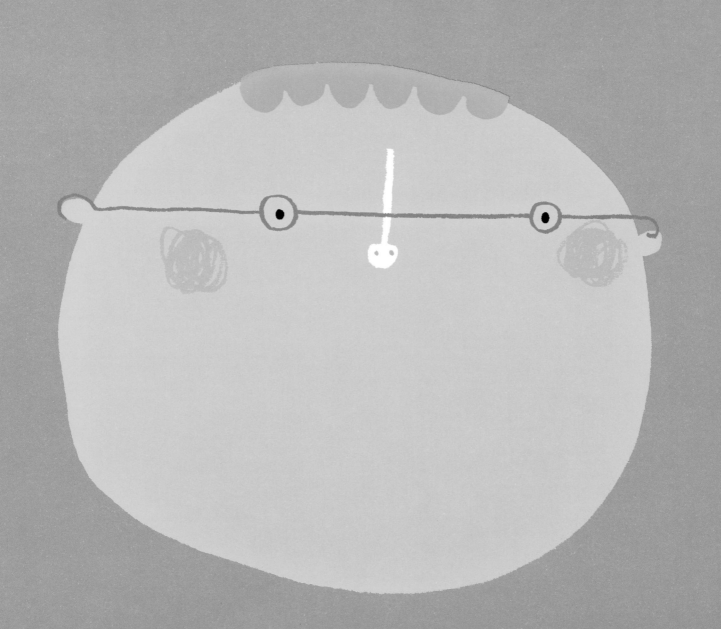

Here is another hole.
Color it in.

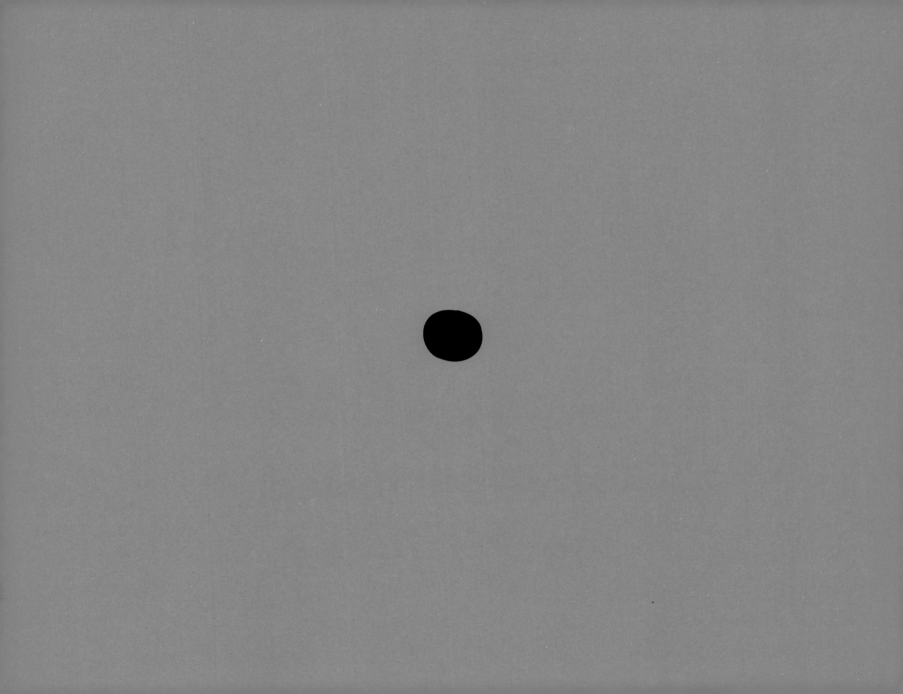

Hey!
Who scribbled
on my nose?

The girl has drawn a round ball.

Draw balloons for all the kids.

Also available from Seven Footer Kids:

www.lazoo.com
www.SevenFooterKids.com

Originally published as "Odekakekun Anaboko Nuru Hon"
©2004 La ZOO / GAKKEN
First published in Japan 2004 by Gakken Co., Ltd.
English translation rights arranged with Gakken Co., Ltd.
through Nextoy, LLC

Published by Seven Footer Kids, an imprint of Seven Footer Press,
a division of Seven Footer Entertainment LLC, NY
Manufactured in Beijing, P.R.China,
in 03/2010 by C&C JOINT PRINTING CO., (BEIJING) LTD
10 9 8 7 6 5 4
© Copyright Seven Footer Kids, 2009 for English Edition
All Rights Reserved
English adaptation designed by Junko Miyakoshi

ISBN 978-1-934734-12-4